Meet the Artist

DAVID HOCKNEY

Illustrated by

Rose Blake

TATE

Daring

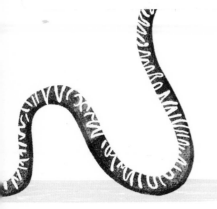

Colourful

Curious

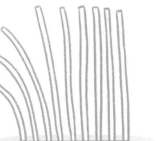

MELROSE AVE.
8200 W ←

Inspired by the world around him, David Hockney uses art to ask the questions — do we really know what things look like? Or, do we just think we do?

Hockney was born in Bradford, UK in 1937. He was passionate about art from an early age, inspired by artists such as Picasso and Matisse. He was educated at Bradford Grammar school and then attended the Regional College of Art, Bradford before being accepted to the prestigious Royal College of Art in London.

In 1964, he left the UK in search of somewhere new and exciting. He ended up in the sunny landscape of Los Angeles, USA.

Throughout his career, Hockney has experimented with different art forms including portraits, landscapes, photocollages, set design and iPad drawings. He has created many great works of art and is regarded as one of the most influential British artists of the twentieth century.

For painting you need three things:

The hand   **The eye**   **The heart**

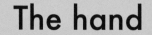
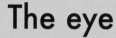

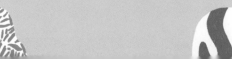
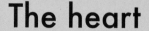

From the rolling hills of Yorkshire to the bright and light scenery of Los Angeles, Hockney has always been interested in the different landscapes around him.

Garrowby Hill is a vibrant and colourful painting of the Yorkshire countryside.

Look at these two paintings together – can you see any similarities?
What are the differences? Which do you prefer and why?

Placed on a map-like background, *Outpost Drive, Hollywood*
shows the wide open spaces of LA.
Write a list of your favourite places to visit!
Why not paint or sketch pictures of these places?

Hockney enjoyed driving through the LA landscape whilst listening to his favourite music. He would often try and suit the music to the scenery around him.

Find your way to Hockney's blue house. You could do it whilst listening to your favourite song.

Colour Wheel

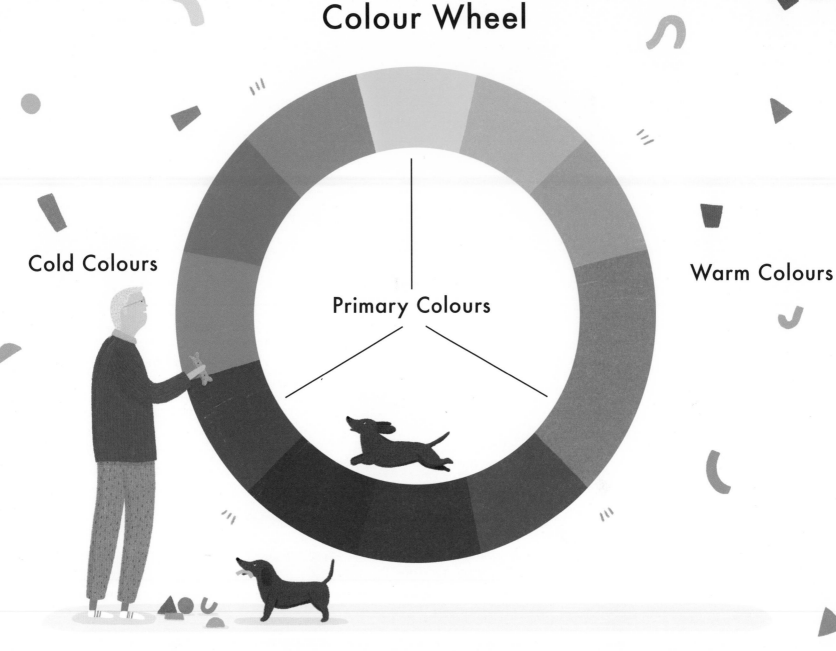

Cold Colours

Warm Colours

Primary Colours

Colour is very important in the bright landscapes painted by Hockney.
Colours can help an artist show location, mood, time and lots
more in their artworks.

The colour wheel above shows which colours
go together and which are contrasting.

Which colours would you use to show these emotions?

Happy	Sad	Angry
Jealous	Excited	Nervous
Shy	Brave	Confident

Create your own Hockney inspired landscape!

1. Paint a horizon line on the page.
2. Now add a river or road in the centre of your painting.
3. Paint lines to divide the rest of the space into smaller areas.
4. Paint each of the small sections in your favourite colours.

Top Tip:
Remember to mix colours to create your own unique shades!

Picasso
CÉZANNE
HOCKNEY

5. Then add texture to your landscape. You can use sponges, stamps or even the end of your paintbrush.

Voila! You now have your very own landscape painting.

A *Rake's Progress* is a series of sixteen prints that tell the story of Hockney's first time in New York.

Why don't you create your own story in pictures – just like a comic-book strip!

Pick an exciting thing that's happened to you, such as a holiday or a great day out!

Plot out your story and then draw it in these sixteen boxes.

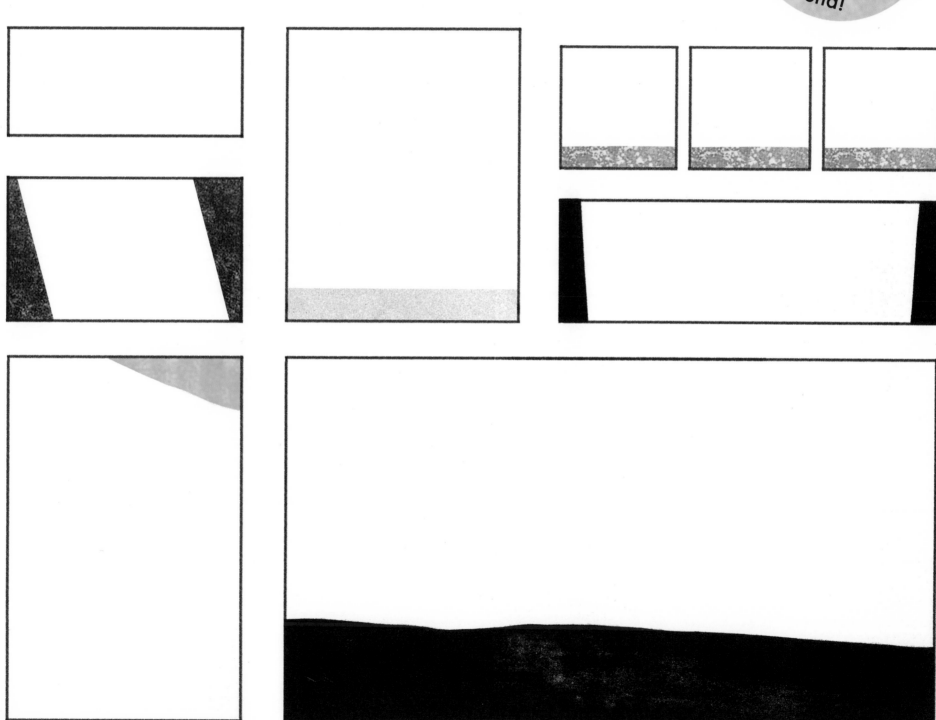

Fascinated by water, Hockney played with
different ways of drawing and painting it.

A *Bigger Splash* is one of Hockney's
most famous paintings.

Try drawing these kinds of water – think about the different textures and colours.

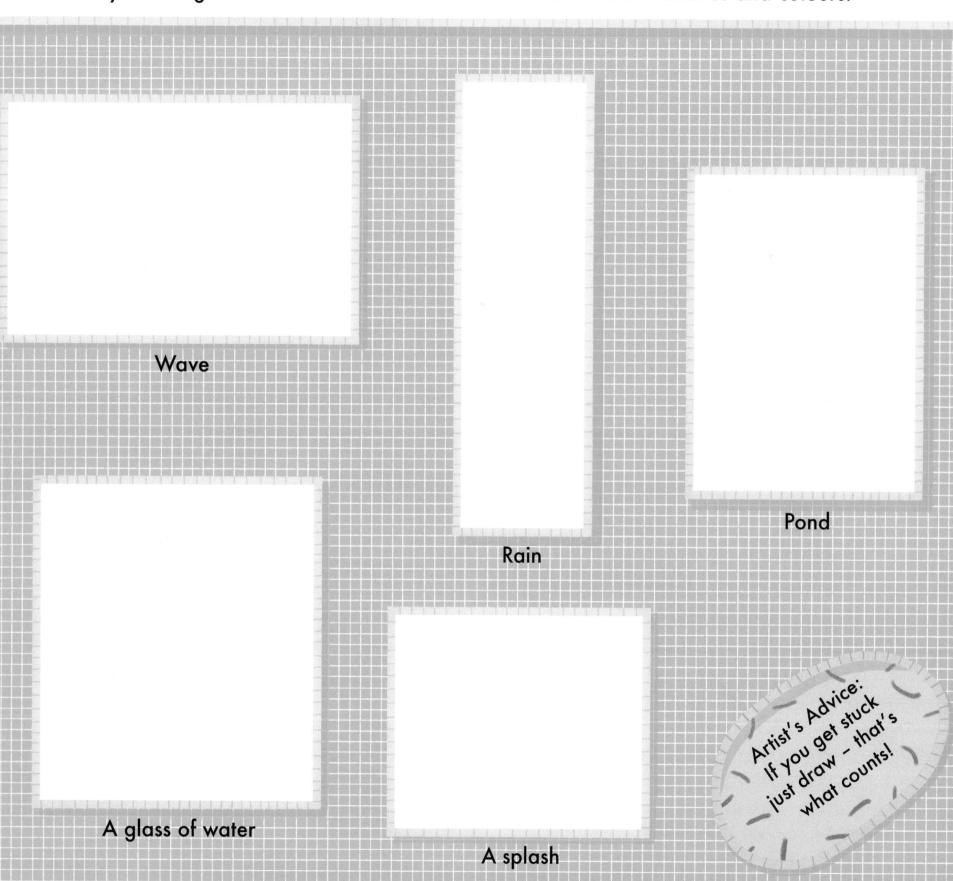

Wave

Rain

Pond

A glass of water

A splash

Artist's Advice:
If you get stuck
just draw – that's
what counts!

Hockney enjoyed experimenting by drawing an object in lots of different ways.

Pick a flower and draw it below.

Now, draw the flower using only three colours.

Draw the flower using only five lines.

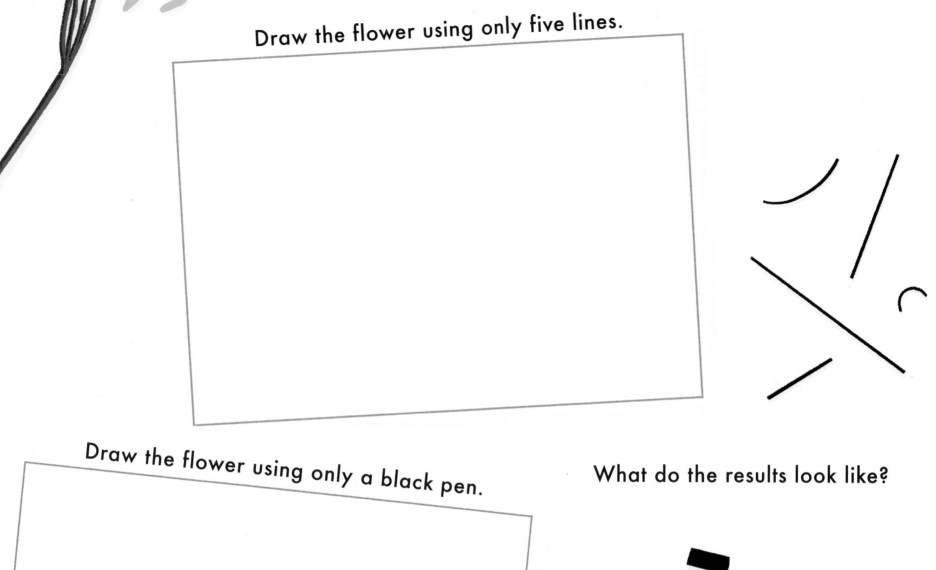

Draw the flower using only a black pen.

What do the results look like?

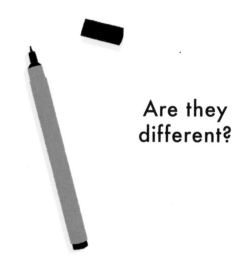

Are they different?

Which do you like best?

Hockney has created a number of stage designs for opera, theatre and ballet productions.

Write your very own play – think about the characters, the plot and the ending.

Then once you're happy, design the ideal stage set for it.

Hockney's first stage design was for an opera called *The Rake's Progress*.

CAFE

tabac BAR

Here are a few key things to think about.
A stage set should:

Tell us where the play is happening — is it inside or outside?
Is it in a wood, or in a castle?

Provide a mood and atmosphere — is the play happy or sad?
Is it scary?

Create a style and tone — is it bright and colourful or dark and mysterious?

Hockney has created portraits of his friends and family throughout his career. He is fascinated by people and finds their faces the most interesting part to paint.

This painting is called *My Parents*. Hockney's mother is watching him painting her and his father is reading a book.

Draw a picture of your family
or your best friend.

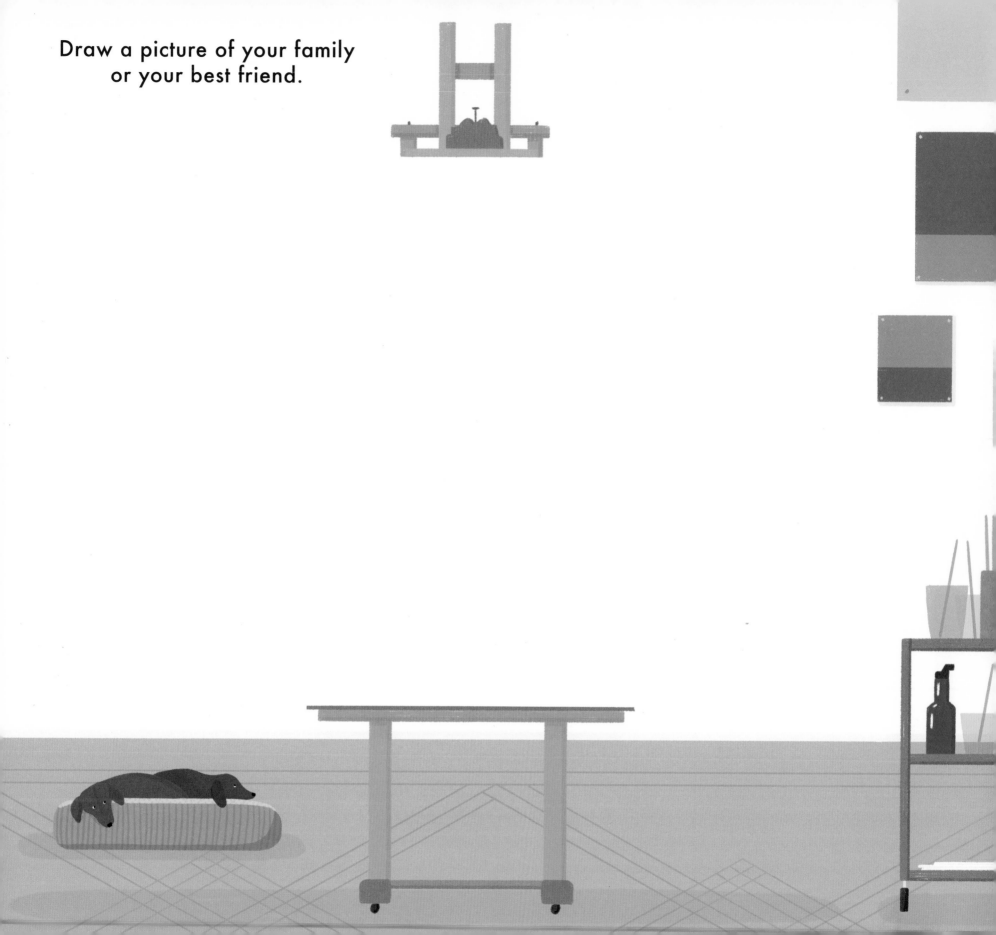

A self-portrait is a picture you draw of yourself!
It's quite a tricky thing to draw, as you can't see yourself easily.
Draw your portrait below with pencil.

It might help to try looking at yourself
in a mirror while you draw.

CALIFORNIA

Now draw it again, but use a different style! You could use paints, pencils, black pens, chalks or photocollage.

SAN FRANCISCO
OPERA

Puccini's
TURANDOT

TOBER 1993 | ADMIT ONE

Which style do you think suits your personality best?

SONG OF MYSELF

In the 1980s, Hockney started to make photocollages. He would take lots of pictures of one thing and then arrange them together to create a larger image – like patchwork.

Pearblossom Hwy. is a photocollage showing a bright and colourful highway in California.

What can you see in this image?

If you look closely, are there things you didn't notice before?

Be sure to look at the background, the middle ground and the foreground!

Create your own photocollage

Top Tip:
Don't be afraid
to experiment!

1.
Pick a subject – it could be your pet,
your best friend or your favourite place.

2.
Take at least thirty pictures
of it from lots of
different angles.

3.
Print out your photos.

4.
Arrange your
photos to create
one large image.
Don't forget to
layer them!

Hockney loves to experiment with new technology and has started to create artworks on his iPad and mobile phone.

Each day, Hockney liked to draw a different bunch of flowers on his mobile phone.

Then he would email them to his friends and family – so they had a fresh bunch of flowers every day!

FROM: DAVID HOCKNEY

Draw a picture of a special gift you would like to give your friends and family each day. It could be the same gift or seven different ones.

You could then take a picture of your drawings and email them to all your friends and family.

Monday

Tuesday	Wednesday	Thursday

Friday	Saturday	Sunday

Let your imagination run wild and draw pictures below to create your very own art collection.

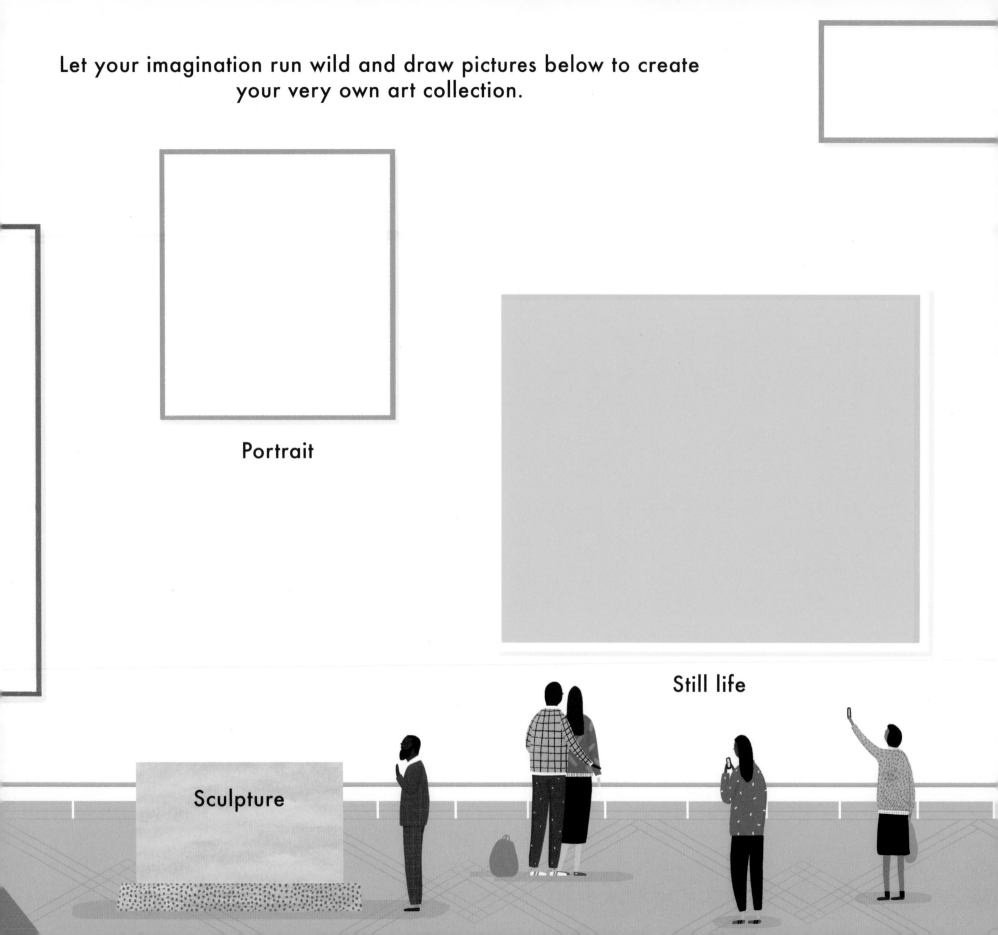

Portrait

Still life

Sculpture

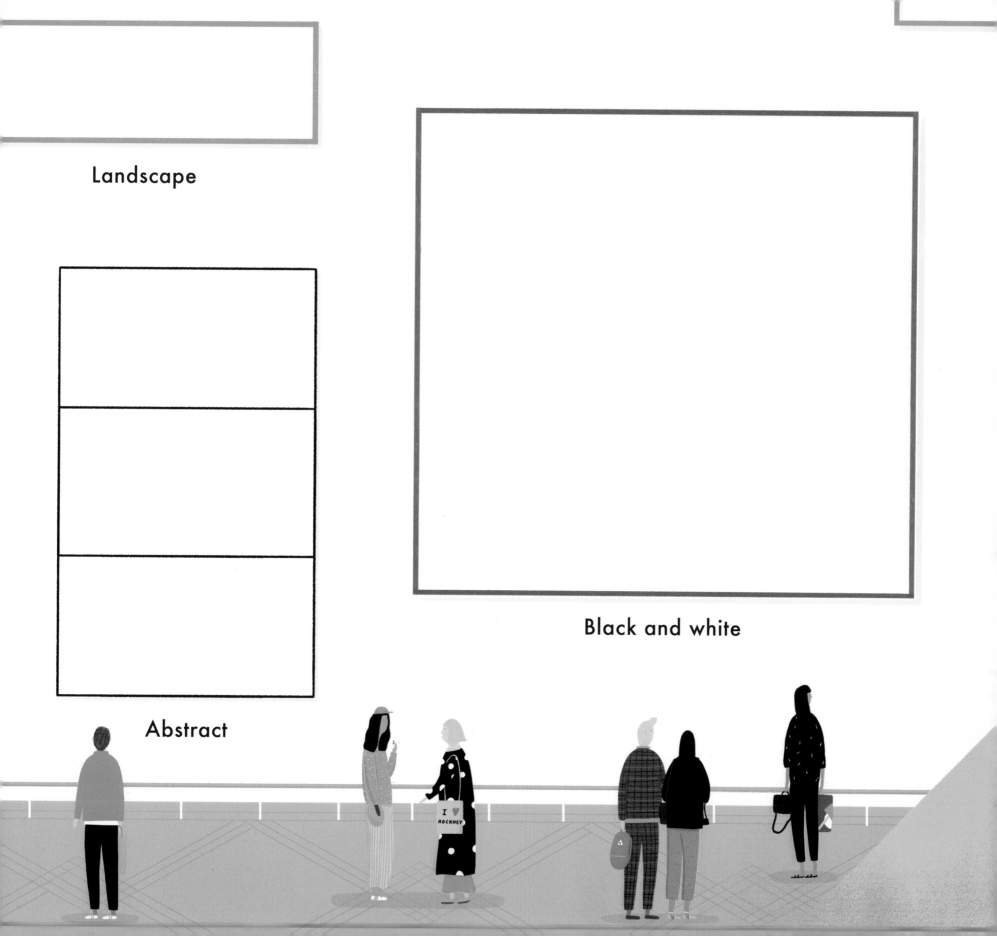

Landscape

Abstract

Black and white

Page 5:
Outpost Drive, Hollywood
1980
Acrylic paint on canvas
152.4 x 152.4
Private Collection

Page 4:
Garrowby Hill
1998
Oil paint on canvas
152.4 x 193
Museum of Fine Arts,
Boston

Page 14:
A Bigger Splash
1967
Acrylic paint on canvas
242.5 x 243.9
Tate

Page 20:
My Parents
1977
Oil paint on canvas
182.9 x 182.9
Tate

Page 24:
Pearblossom Hwy., 11-18th April 1986 #1
1986
Photographic collage
128 x 171.8
J. Paul Getty Museum, Los Angeles

Page 26:
Shoes, 3 September 2010 (384)
2010
iPad drawing
Collection of the Artist

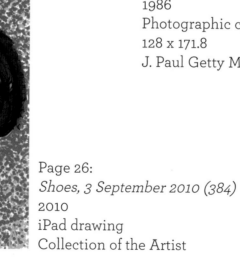

With special thanks to
David Hockney, Inc

First published 2017 by order of the Tate Trustees
by Tate Publishing, a division of Tate Enterprises Ltd,
Millbank, London SW1P 4RG
www.tate.org.uk/publishing

Reprinted 2017, 2018

A catalogue record for this book is available from the British Library

ISBN 978 1 84976 446 9

Distributed in the United States and Canada by ABRAMS, New York
Library of Congress Control Number applied for

Designed by Nous Vous
Colour reproduction by DL Imaging, London
Printed and bound by Litografia Rosés / SYL L'Art Grafic, Spain

Measurements of artworks are given in centimetres, height before width